THE 2011
JAPAN DISASTERS

Essential Events

THE 2011
JAPAN DISASTERS

BY MARCIA AMIDON LUSTED

Content Consultant
Ethan Isaac Segal
Associate Professor of History
Michigan State University

ABDO
Publishing Company

CREDITS

Published by ABDO Publishing Company, 8000 West 78th Street, Edina, Minnesota 55439. Copyright © 2012 by Abdo Consulting Group, Inc. International copyrights reserved in all countries. No part of this book may be reproduced in any form without written permission from the publisher. The Essential Library™ is a trademark and logo of ABDO Publishing Company.

Printed in the United States of America,
North Mankato, Minnesota
082011
092011

 THIS BOOK CONTAINS AT LEAST 10% RECYCLED MATERIALS.

Editor: Mari Kesselring
Copy Editor: Paula Lewis
Cover Design: Becky Daum
Interior Design and Production: Kazuko Collins

Library of Congress Cataloging-in-Publication Data
Lusted, Marcia Amidon.
  The 2011 Japan disasters / Marcia Amidon Lusted.
      p. cm. -- (Essential events)
  Includes bibliographical references and index.
  ISBN 978-1-61783-179-9
  1. Earthquakes--Japan--Juvenile literature. 2. Tsunamis--Japan--Juvenile literature. 3. Tohoku Earthquake and Tsunami, Japan, 2011--Juvenile literature. I. Title.
  QE537.2.J3L85 2012
  952.0512--dc23
                                    2011023856

TABLE OF CONTENTS

This submerged car was one of many swept to sea during the quake-triggered tsunami.

March 11, 2011

*I*t was a normal Friday afternoon in the offices of a Tokyo, Japan, Internet company that occupied the tenth floor of a high-rise building. No one was particularly concerned by the tremors of an earthquake. A frequent occurrence in

Tokyo, earthquakes usually lasted only 30 seconds and caused little or no damage. Ken Saito was in his office when the shaking began:

> We were all laughing at first, thinking it was a regular earthquake. A lot of people were, you know, taking videos on their cell phones, and a lot of people were saying, it's going to end soon. But once it got serious, you know, we can see their expressions change on their faces. There were a lot of people screaming, so people started going under their desks. And it really, literally, went on for maybe two minutes. . . . And I'm not exaggerating when I'm saying I thought—I seriously thought I was going to die, because it was that big. I never felt anything that big before. There was a big sway going on for a long time. When we looked outside the window, we can see that the scenery was moving because the building was shaking, so that was really scary.[1]

It soon became clear that this was no ordinary earthquake, even in a country that was accustomed to frequent tremors and shaking. An American who had been living in Tokyo for several years said, "You could tell this was different instantly from the other little tremors we've had before. It just picked up in intensity."[2] Grant Stillman, a reporter for the *Australian Sydney Morning Herald*, said, "From my building, I watched skyscrapers sway like the masts of yachts. My building started making cracking sounds under our feet and that's when we took to the staircase."[3]

Ultimately, this earthquake registered 9.0 on the Richter scale. It was one of the largest earthquakes ever recorded and the biggest earthquake ever to hit Japan. And the quake would only be the beginning.

A Wall of Water

Within an hour after the approximately five-minute earthquake finally stopped, officials issued a tsunami warning. The warning went out not only to Japan, but to 50 other countries including the West Coast of the United States. A tsunami is a series of huge waves that are created offshore by the movement of undersea earthquakes or volcanoes, and then move toward land. The waves move outward in

The Richter Scale

The Richter scale is a tool developed by scientists to classify the size of earthquakes. The scale ranges from 1 to 10 and indicates the total amount of energy released by the quake. Each number represents a force ten times greater than the number below it. For example, any quake over a reading of 6 is considered severe, but a quake that measures 7 on the Richter scale is ten times stronger than a quake with a magnitude of 6.

Coastal cities such as Yamada in Iwate Prefecture were left in ruins.

concentric rings and can affect any area whose coast touches the body of water where the tsunami began. The waves often reach incredible heights as they crash onto the shore and drag everything in their path back toward the sea. Japan's earthquake spawned a tsunami with waves more than 30 feet (9 m) high. Some of the waves washed inland six miles (10 km) from the coast. Within just a few minutes of the wave's appearance, the damage was widespread. Cars, boats, and trains were swept away. Bridges and roads collapsed. Houses were destroyed.

Masaki Ohata was in Kesennuma City when the tsunami struck. He risked his life for his dog, Shell:

When the tsunami hit, I was in a car trying to evacuate with my mother and my dog. . . . The waters came so quickly that I could feel the car start to float. I couldn't open the door so I climbed through the window, pulled my mother out and tried to get Shell to leave. But he was too scared. The car started to sink so I lunged in and heaved the dog into the water. We all swam together until the water subsided.[4]

Saving Lives

Takeshi Kanno was a doctor at Shizugawa Public Hospital in the Japanese town of Minami Sanriku. He was on duty when the earthquake struck and the tsunami warning sirens sounded. Kanno immediately started moving hospital patients out of the lower floors of the hospital onto the highest floor where they would be safer. In the short amount of time between the quake and the tsunami, he moved dozens of patients to safety. When the tsunami struck, he watched as it swallowed the street below in just three minutes. When Kanno and his coworkers returned to the lower floors to find those who they had not been able to move, he found they were all gone—swept out of the building with the tsunami waves.

Kanno remained with his patients for the next two days, waiting until all of his patients were evacuated by helicopter before leaving. He returned home just in time for the birth of his second child, a boy. They named him Rei, which in Japanese means "the wisdom to overcome hardship." *Time* magazine named Takeshi Kanno one of its 100 Most Influential People of 2011 because of the lives he saved on March 11, 2011.

Many others in Kesennuma City drowned in their cars when the tsunami wave engulfed a huge traffic jam of people trying to flee. A reporter for Bloomberg television witnessed the destruction, "[The wave] was mixed with mud, with ships and cars smashing toward wooden houses, dragging those into rice fields, and basically bashing them into pieces."[5]

The tsunami crippled Japan's Sendai Airport, coating its runways with a thick layer of mud and leaving cars, trucks, and buses behind. Fires broke out in the rubble left by the earthquake and the tsunami. The Cosmo Oil Refinery in Ichihara, 40 miles (64 km) outside Tokyo, caught fire and burned out of control. Witnesses reported seeing 100-foot (30-m) flames leaping into the sky.

Lost and Found

Many people lost family members and friends in the earthquake and tsunami. In many cases, they did not know if their loved ones were still alive. In the city hall at Kesennuma City, which was extensively damaged by the tsunami waves, people sought information on loved ones' whereabouts. "The corridor of the city hall has become a lost-and-found centre for human beings. On one side is the 'seeking' wall, which is home to hundreds of neatly written requests for information on missing persons; opposite is the 'refugee' wall, which lists the names of those staying at the dozen or so evacuation centres around Kesennuma."[6]

And a Volcano, Too

In addition to the major earthquake and devastating tsunami, Japan also experienced a volcanic eruption two days after the tsunami. The Shinmoedake volcano, located in the Kirishima range on the southern Kyushu island in southwestern Japan, sent plumes of ash and smoke into the air. It scattered rock and broke windows as far as four miles (6 km) away. Hot ash rained down over surrounding areas as people evacuated. Officials feared a worse eruption would occur as a lava dome formed within the volcano's crater, but as of July 2011, no further incidents had taken place.

STILL SHAKING

As if the initial earthquake was not enough, aftershocks continued to jar Japan in the following days. More than 50 aftershocks continued in the wake of the first quake, and seven of those measured at least 6.3 on the Richter scale. Many of these aftershocks were damaging in their own right. Canadian photographer Andrew Pateras wrote in his blog on the night of the first earthquake:

> *I am writing to you at after midnight Tokyo time and the aftershocks are still hitting hard. The best way to describe it is to compare it to being in your cabin on a cruise ship during a storm. I am on dry land and I am actually feeling sea sick. . . . I have lived through many life changing events, but this one will be forever burned in my memory.*[7]

A Nuclear Emergency

The destruction caused by the quake and the tsunami had an even more devastating impact. Several of Japan's 54 nuclear power plants were affected by the disaster. Many were unable to sufficiently cool their nuclear reactors after their electricity and generators were knocked out by the quake and the tsunami's flooding. The four plants closest to the center of the quake were shut down early Friday evening. But the cooling system at the Fukushima Daiichi Nuclear Power Station on Japan's northeast coast failed. Officials declared a state of emergency at the plant and began evacuating people who lived within six miles (10 km) of the plant. As days passed, the situation at Fukushima worsened.

By Friday evening, the first estimates of the loss of lives were reported. Hundreds were already

Miracle Story

In the village of Ishinomaki, a town on the coast northeast of Sendai, a deadly tsunami wave crashed into a family home, ripping a four-month-old baby girl from her parents' arms. Three days later, soldiers searching the area for survivors thought they heard crying. They crawled through the debris and found the missing baby girl. The baby was unharmed. Both of her parents survived the tsunami as well.

known to be dead, and that number would soon rise to the thousands. Ten thousand were missing just from one town alone, Minamisanriku, located on the coast. Thousands more were missing. Millions of households had no water or power. The possibility of radiation being released from damaged nuclear plants increased. Japan's prime minister called it the country's worst crisis since World War II. ⌒

The fiery explosion at the Cosmo oil refinery in Ichihara was one of many casualties left in the wake of the tsunami.

Japan has a history of earthquakes. An earthquake in Tokyo in 1923 left part of the city damaged by the earthquake and the resulting fires.

A History of Disaster

As devastating as the 2011 earthquake was, Japan is no stranger to disasters, many of which have been caused by earthquakes and tsunamis. In the nineteenth century, several earthquakes and volcanic eruptions struck the island country and generated tsunami waves that killed thousands of people.

Honshu and Kanto

One of Japan's significant disasters occurred in 1896 when a magnitude 7.2 earthquake rumbled beneath the ocean floor approximately 120 miles (193 km) off the coast of the island of Honshu. The quake was not big enough to cause real alarm, especially in a country where earthquakes were frequent. A quake this size did not usually generate a tsunami. However, it struck in relatively shallow water and lasted for almost two minutes, which created a huge tsunami. Waves towering as high as 125 feet (38 m) made their way inland. Author Christine Gibson described the destruction:

> People celebrating on the beach suddenly noticed the water receding. Then they heard a hiss, like oncoming rain. Most

The Shindo Scale

While most of the world measures earthquakes according to the Richter scale, the Japanese more commonly use the Shindo scale. The Shindo scale measures the intensity of an earthquake at a specific location, which is what people feel at a specific place. The Richter scale measures the actual energy released by an earthquake at its epicenter. The Shindo scale ranges from 0 to 7. Shindo 1 is a slight earthquake felt by people who are not moving, while Shindo 7 is a severe earthquake.

of them were killed instantly. . . . In most cases, officials found it simpler to calculate village death tolls by subtracting the number of survivors from the population rather than adding up all the dead. Villagers, using fishing nets, pulled the dead from the ocean by the scores.[1]

But the Honshu earthquake and tsunami was not the worst disaster in Japanese history. In 1923, a quake struck the Kanto plain near Tokyo and killed more than 100,000 people. The earthquake happened around lunchtime. Many people were at home cooking lunch on fires and stoves. When the earthquake hit, many buildings, most of them made of wood and paper, were set ablaze. A report in a British newspaper conveyed the aftermath:

The terror inspired by the repeated shocks and the falling of houses was magnified by the breaking out of fires in all directions, and at Yokohama and other points on the Bay of Tokyo by the inrush of [tsunami waves]. Bridges fell and railways were snapped and twisted out of shape. It is said that one or two islands in the Bay much frequented by summer visitors disappeared and that new islands rose to the surface.[2]

The Kanto earthquake was the worst in modern Japanese history, but another terrible earthquake with a magnitude of 7.2 struck the city of Kobe on

January 17, 1995. More than 6,000 people died and 300,000 lost their homes.

LOCATION, LOCATION, LOCATION

Japan is located at a point where four of the huge plates that make up Earth's crust come together and collide, which makes the island nation vulnerable to earthquakes and the tsunamis that often follow. This area is called a subduction zone. These plates move constantly, grinding past each other across surfaces known as faults. The friction of movement makes these plates deform slightly, and they store up energy like a spring. When that friction suddenly gives way and the plates slip, the stored energy is released as an earthquake. Because of Japan's location so close to this subduction zone, it frequently experiences earthquakes.

Tsunamis, which are usually generated by an earthquake, are sometimes confused with tidal waves. But tidal waves are simply abnormally large waves caused by the interaction of the natural ocean

A Deadly Trap

Part of what makes a tsunami so deadly is that it can be very deceiving. The water at the shore may bubble or even pull away from the beach. People often become curious when large areas of the ocean floor are suddenly exposed. Rushing out to look and to pick up shells and fish, people become trapped by the sudden oncoming tsunami wave. When a tsunami reaches land, it is almost impossible to outswim or outrun.

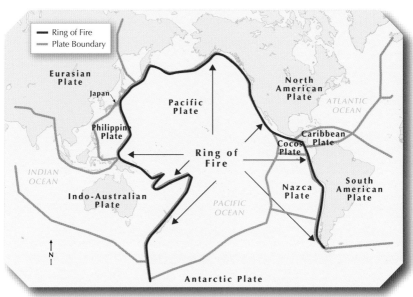

Japan's coast is part of an area called the Ring of Fire.

tides with the forces of the sun, moon, or wind.
A tsunami—which is a Japanese word that means
"harbor wave"—occurs when a large quantity of water
in the ocean is suddenly displaced. A tsunami is like
dropping a rock into a puddle and creating rings that
travel outward from the point where the rock hit. A
disturbance such as an earthquake, an underwater
volcanic eruption, or a landslide can displace a large
quantity of water suddenly and send it toward land.
These waves move quickly and often grow in intensity
as they approach land.

Japan's location near tectonic plates is not the only reason why it is vulnerable to tsunamis. It is located in a geologic area known as the Ring of Fire. This area is a horseshoe-shaped zone that partially surrounds the Pacific Ocean basin. Because of the tectonic plates, the region has many volcanoes and ocean trenches as well as thousands of miles of faults. As a result, the Ring of Fire is home to more than half of the world's volcanoes. Almost all of the world's major earthquakes also occur in this region.

BEING PREPARED

Because of the seismic activity in the Ring of Fire, the Pacific Tsunami Warning Center was established in 1968 to monitor earthquake and tsunami activity. The center sends out warnings to areas that might be in the path of a tsunami.

Japan, however, has taken earthquake and tsunami preparedness even further. After the 1923 Kanto earthquake, buildings were rebuilt using concrete and steel instead of materials that could be destroyed

The 2004 Tsunami

One of the worst tsunamis in modern times struck the Indian Ocean in December 2004. An earthquake off the coast of Indonesia created a tsunami. Its waves damaged 14 countries—particularly Indonesia, Thailand, India, and Sri Lanka—and killed more than 200,000 people.

by fire. Building codes were updated again in 1981 to specifically make buildings more earthquake proof. Skyscrapers are specially constructed to sway with the moving ground rather than collapse. Earthquake- and tsunami-proof shelters have been created on the east coast of Japan where tsunamis most frequently strike. Some cities have built tsunami walls and floodgates to keep tsunami waves from traveling inland through rivers.

Japan also has one of the most sophisticated earthquake warning systems in the

Waves

The difference between a normal ocean wave and a tsunami wave is their wavelengths. The wavelength is the distance from the crest, or top, of one wave to the crest of the next wave. A wave loses energy as it travels, and the amount of energy it loses depends on its wavelength. A normal ocean wave is created by wind. It has a short wavelength and loses its energy quickly. A tsunami wave, however, has a very long wavelength. As a result, a tsunami wave does not lose energy as quickly as it travels. While a normal ocean wave may reach the shore with very little energy left, a tsunami wave will still have a great deal of energy. A tsunami wave begins to drag and slow down when it reaches shallower water near the shore. As it slows, the water behind the wave is still moving quickly and piles up against the tsunami wave. As a result, the height of the tsunami wave increases. The wave height also depends on the coastline. If the ocean floor slopes up to the shore at a steep angle, the tsunami wave will slow more quickly and pile up faster and higher. If there is a gentle slope from ocean to shore, the wave slows more gradually and will not be as high. That is why tsunami waves can vary from 30 feet (9 m) to more than 100 feet (30 m) in height by the time they reach land.

world as well as a tsunami warning system with 300 sensors set up around the country. The Japan Meteorological Agency's monitoring center follows earthquakes and tsunamis 24 hours a day. The nation also launched an online warning system in 2007. Using seismographs that measure movement in the ground, automatic warnings are sent out to factories, schools, television stations, radio stations, and mobile phones. Japanese schoolchildren are taught to distinguish between the two kinds of waves that travel through the ground: primary and secondary. Primary, or P, waves occur first and do little damage, but are followed by secondary, or S, waves, which inflict the most damage. By learning to identify P waves, citizens know that an S wave will follow and can prepare or head for safer areas. Even a few extra minutes might be enough to save a life.

However, Japan's extraordinary warnings and preparedness systems could not cope with the strong quake of March 11, 2011. The initial quake, coupled with more than 100 aftershocks that were as strong

Disaster Prevention Day

Since 1960, Japan has held Disaster Prevention Day on September 1, the anniversary of the 1923 Tokyo earthquake. Schools, fire stations, and public and private facilities hold evacuation drills for fires and earthquakes. Children practice putting on *bosai zukkin*, protective padded headgear, which they use as seat cushions at normal times.

as many major earthquakes, was more damaging than anything experienced before in Japan. It also occurred in a part of the subduction zone that was thought to be less likely to spawn an earthquake. Even with a population that was well educated about earthquakes and tsunamis, there was not enough time to get people out of the path of the tsunami waves.

Survivors at an evacuation center in Iwate Prefecture scan a list of people missing following the earthquake and tsunami.

After the earthquake, many trains and subways stopped running. People who were at work in downtown Tokyo had to walk miles to their homes.

AFTER THE EARTH SHOOK

he earthquake that struck Japan on March 11, 2011, lasted approximately five minutes. When it was over, Japan's coastline had moved and changed the balance of the planet. Portions of northern Japan were now almost eight feet (2 m) closer to North America than they had been before the quake. The global positioning stations that were located the closest to the epicenter of the quake moved eastward as much as 13 feet (4 m). According to a *New York Times* report, "NASA scientists calculated that the redistribution of mass by the earthquake might have shortened the day by a couple of millionths of a second and tilted the Earth's axis slightly."[1]

In the cities, the earthquake roared and rumbled, shaking buildings, knocking over furniture, and heaving and buckling the surfaces of highways. Immediately after the quake, in cities such as Tokyo, people scrambled out of high-rise buildings to seek shelter. Many evacuees gathered in parks, afraid to reenter buildings. Subways were closed and train service was shut down; many workers set off to walk to their homes. For as long as 18 hours after the

Stranded in the City

Guardian newspaper's blog reported on Saturday morning, "In Tokyo, office workers who were stranded in the city after the quake forced the subway system to close early slept alongside the homeless at one station. Scores of men in suits lay on newspapers, using their briefcases as pillows. At least 116,000 people in Tokyo had been unable to return home on Friday evening due to transport disruption."[2]

quake, thousands of people, still dressed in work clothes, were struggling to reach their homes from the central business district. David S. Abrahams, an American living in Tokyo, described the scene:

Most people who work here live more than an hour away by train. But Tokyo's trains had stopped running, and the highways were closed. Helicopters roared aimlessly above; police sirens blared and lines of people waited for buses that never appeared to come. Normally empty taxis never had a better day. Although many people were armed with maps, it was not clear where they were going. [3]

The Statistics

The epicenter of the earthquake, which came to be known as the Tohoku Earthquake, was located approximately 45 miles (72 km) east of the Oshika Peninsula of Tohoku, and 15 miles (24 km) below the earth's surface. Sendai, the nearest city, was located on the island of Honshu, 80 miles (129 km) from the quake's epicenter. The quake was 232 miles (373 km) northeast of Tokyo.

The quake occurred at 2:46 p.m. in Japan and lasted approximately five minutes. Foreshocks had been felt for several days before the quake, and more than 800 aftershocks occurred as of May 2011. Scientists suggest these aftershocks may continue for years. The Tohoku Earthquake first registered as a magnitude of 7.9. It was then upgraded to 8.8, then 8.9, and was finally designated at 9.0. This makes it one of the five most powerful earthquakes to have occurred since modern record keeping began in 1900. As of July 2011, the number of people dead or missing had risen to more than 22,000.

In the suburbs around Tokyo, some buildings had been constructed on reclaimed land, meaning land that was created by filling wet areas. The quake caused areas of this reclaimed land to liquefy, destroying some homes and buildings and damaging even more.

However, those in the southern cities were luckier than many in the northeast part of the country, which was closer to the quake's epicenter. Thousands of homes had been destroyed, many roads were impassable, and three trains were known to be missing. Cell phone reception and electric power were down. People desperately looked for missing family members.

In Sendai, which suffered most heavily from the quake, the members of the Monkey Majik rock band tweeted through the night about what was happening around them:

The Sound of the Quake

Scientists at the National Oceanic and Atmospheric Administration Vents Program at Pacific Marine Environmental Laboratory and Oregon State University were able to hear the sound of the Japan earthquake as it took place, through a hydrophone, which is an underwater microphone. This was the largest sound ever heard over the hydrophone.

Just walked outside, completely different feel from last night . . . lights on all over the city . . . very calm . . . still getting tremors . . . the whole city smells like fire! You can see the smoke from the gas plant down the road. Keeping positive, but so many people have been injured, or killed.[4]

Kumi Onodera, a dental technician from Sendai, was quoted in a blog for the British newspaper *Guardian*:

[Kumi] compared the earthquake and aftermath to "a scene from a disaster movie." Described the tremor as being so intense that the ground in Sendai began rippling. "The road was moving up and down like a wave. Things were on fire and it was 'snowing' [debris and ash]." People were trying hard to be positive, she said, but it was difficult. "You come to appreciate what you have in your everyday life. Everything is so hard now."[5]

Conserving Power

As early as the morning after the quake, officials used Tokyo's public address system to advise residents to conserve electricity by turning off nonessential appliances. The government was worried about power outages caused by damage to and destruction of power plants.

An aerial view of Sendai shows the extreme destruction caused by the disaster.

The First Days

By the morning after the quake, Japanese officials feared the death toll would soon rise to the thousands. In Sendai alone, a port city close to the quake's epicenter, approximately 300 bodies had already been found along the waterline.

The country quickly set disaster plans in motion. Rescue teams assembled to look for survivors and to free those who had been trapped by the quake's damage or the resulting tsunami. The teams also rushed supplies such as food and water to those who had none and were without heat and telephones. More than 800 people were rescued from an elementary school and another 1,200 from a junior high school. They had had no food or water. The Japanese newspaper, *Mainichi Shimbun*, reported that 600 people had taken shelter on the roof of a public school in Sendai. The Japanese Self-Defense Force evacuated them. The *New York Times* reported:

> *On the rooftop of Chuo Hospital in the city of Iwanuma, doctors and nurses were waving white flags and pink umbrellas, according to TV Asahi. On the floor of the roof, they wrote "Help" in English, and "Food" in Japanese. The reporter, observing the scene from a helicopter, said, "If anyone in the City Hall office is watching, please help them."*[6]

Finding the Missing Virtually

Just a few days after the Japan earthquake and tsunami, Google launched Google Crisis Response, which includes a Person Finder application to help people find missing relatives and friends. The site also includes links to national and international aid groups, shelter information, disaster message boards, alerts, and transportation statuses.

Survivors in Natori in Miyagi Prefecture evacuated the town.

People continued searching for missing family members. Fumiaki Yamato, who had been in his second home in a mountain village outside Sendai, tried to drive into the city to find the rest of his family. The trip usually took an hour, but now many parts of the road were impassable. "I'm getting worried," he told a reporter by phone. "I don't know how many hours it's going to take."[7]

By Sunday, March 13, the Japanese government had ordered 100,000 troops to provide relief in the worst of the quake-damaged areas. Three hundred planes and 40 ships also were mobilized for search and rescue missions as the list of people unaccounted for continued to grow. However, the damage and destruction caused just by the earthquake began to seem minor when compared to the devastation caused by the tsunami waves. It was soon apparent that the death toll was going to be much higher than originally thought. ⌒

Rescuers in Iwate Prefecture search for survivors among the debris.

Members of Japan's Self-Defense Force search for missing people in Higashi Matsushima, Miyagi Prefecture.

SWEPT OUT TO SEA

Japan's earthquake even caused damage hundreds of miles away from the epicenter. But it was the tsunami waves, which swept the coast for hours, that ultimately caused the greatest amount of damage and loss of life.

A WALL OF WATER

The earthquake triggered a tsunami wave that was approximately 30 feet (9 m) tall, making its way to the coast of Japan. Those who lived in flat agricultural areas had no higher ground to run to. The areas hardest hit by the tsunami were in Miyagi and Iwate Prefectures on the northeast coast of Japan, including the region's largest city, Sendai. As the huge wave, generated by the displacement of water over the earthquake's epicenter, washed inland, it picked up debris, houses, cars, trees, and anything else it could sweep away. The water carried everything in its path and shoved it inland. Cars and trucks were tossed around, and soil gave the water a thick, muddy consistency. Ships were lifted out of the water and deposited on land. The runways at Sendai Airport were covered with mud and vehicles were pushed in with the rush of water.

Local and Distant Tsunamis

Tsunamis are categorized in one of two different types of waves, according to the speed at which they travel. A distant tsunami travels outward across the deep ocean. While it only forms a small hump of water, it travels very fast, often from 300 to 500 miles per hour (483 to 805 km/h). A local tsunami wave moves toward shore, and as it does, it slows to speeds of only tens of miles per hour. This forces the waves to become higher and steeper and hit the shoreline with a massive amount of energy.

Fires started in some houses as gas pipes burst. In the city of Ichihara, an oil refinery was lit ablaze. One hundred-foot (30-m) flames rose from the refinery. Much of the destruction was captured on live television.

Those in the path of the tsunami had only seconds to flee. Those who could not outrun the tsunami were swept away and drowned or injured by the debris. The *Boston Glove* described the story of Mary Caitlen Churchill, an American teaching English in Shizugawa, Japan:

The tsunami wave did come though, coursing up fast, first

Sanriku Tsunami, 1896

The Honshu earthquake of 1896 unleashed a devastating tsunami that affected not only Japan, but other areas as well. The tsunami was barely noticeable to the fishermen who were out at sea at the time. According to the US Geological Survey Web site:

Fishermen twenty miles [32 km] out to sea didn't notice the wave pass under their boats because it only had a height at the time of about fifteen inches [38 km]. They were totally unprepared for the devastation that awaited them when they returned to the port of Sanriku. Twenty-eight thousand people were killed and 170 miles [274 km] of coastline were destroyed by the wave that had passed under them.[1]

The tsunami wave reached approximately 80 feet (25 m) by the time it crashed onto the shore, sweeping away every person and building in its path. This tsunami also reached Hawaii where it demolished wharves and swept away buildings. It continued eastward and hit San Francisco, California, with a height of more than 9 feet (3 m). The Sanriku tsunami became the event that sparked serious research into tsunamis in Japan.

through the school's driveway, then the school, then toward the grassy pitch they were all standing on. "We all just ran for the hill behind the school as fast as we could," Churchill said, adding that she didn't look back and that teachers were helping pull people up the steep slope as the brown water full of debris surged toward them. "A couple of people didn't make it. A student. A teacher."[2]

SEARCHING FOR SURVIVORS

The devastation caused by the tsunami made it difficult for rescue teams to search for survivors. Many had taken refuge on the roofs of taller buildings as the tsunami flooded their towns and cities. Early on, it was clear many more bodies would be found. Many who were drowned by the tsunami were then swept out to sea when the wave receded and their bodies returned to land with the tides. Police reported finding approximately 200 to 300 bodies in Sendai just hours after the tsunami, but officials feared the actual number of dead would be in the thousands. Rescuers would continue to search for survivors in the days to come.

Hiromitsu Shinkawa waves to the Maritime Self-Defense Force just before being rescued. The 60-year-old man floated on the roof of his house for two days after the tsunami hit his town.

A Circle of Destruction

The tsunami waves spread out in concentric rings from the earthquake's center, affecting countries located around the Pacific Ocean that were untouched by the quake. The Pacific Tsunami Warning Center activated its tsunami warning system and sent out warnings to places in the Pacific Rim such as Chile, Hawaii, Mexico, and the Pacific coast of the United States. Tsunami waves can travel as quickly as 500 miles per hour (805 km/h) and can be difficult to anticipate. The first tsunami wave that reaches a location may not be the strongest or biggest wave. Waves heights cannot be predicted because they vary according to coastal features. The time between one wave and the next may be as little as five minutes or as long as an hour.

The Pacific Tsunami Warning Center issued a forecast of the expected speed of the tsunami waves that originated in Japan. It established an expected timeline predicting when these waves would reach specific areas. The center calculated the tsunami would strike Hawaii eight hours after the earthquake and expected it to arrive in Chile nearly 24 hours after the quake. While the waves did not heavily damage Hawaii or California, they did cause some deaths in

Ten Miles Out

Two days after the tsunami waves swept the coast of Japan, 60-year-old Hiromitsu Shinkawa from Fukushima Prefecture was found ten miles (16 km) out at sea, clinging to the roof of his destroyed house. Shinkawa had been swept away by the tsunami when he went back to his house to grab his belongings. In just minutes, he was floating out to sea and spent two days clinging to the debris and waving a red flag he managed to make. He was spotted by a ship taking part in rescue efforts. Shinkawa said, "No helicopters or boats that came nearby noticed me, I thought that day was going to be the last day of my life."[3] Unfortunately, his wife, who had been with him when the tsunami hit, was not found.

countries around the Pacific Rim as well as damaging floods.

SAFETY AFTER THE TSUNAMI

Those who survived the tsunami and flooding in Japan struggled to find shelter. Most had lost their homes. There was no power or heat in many cities. Food and water were in short supply.

In Kesennuma, a town of 70,000 residents in Miyagi Prefecture, almost the entire town was on fire and firefighters were unable to put it out. In other towns, residents continued to huddle on rooftops, waiting for rescue. Churchill, after escaping from the tsunami waters engulfing her school, looked for shelter with her colleagues as it began snowing. They spent the night in a building with no more than half a rice ball to eat and no water. The bitterly cold and windy weather made conditions

A Little Good News

Three weeks after the tsunami struck, a dog was rescued by the Japanese Coast Guard. He was found adrift on wreckage approximately one mile (2 km) out at sea from the town of Kesennuma. Once the dog was spotted, Japanese Coast Guard members tried to approach it and rescue it, but the dog evaded them. It took them several hours to capture it and wrap it in a blanket. The dog was wary at first, but once on board the boat, it began licking its rescuers' hands.

even worse for those without food, water, or heated shelters. By March 15, approximately 400,000 people were staying in makeshift shelters and evacuation centers. The number of dead and missing continued to climb as, over the next few days, thousands of bodies that had been washed out to sea were washed back onto shore.

As the days dragged on, stunned and shocked residents of coastal cities tried to find missing family members. They sought food and water. Many also needed gasoline so they could leave the area. Entire towns had disappeared beneath the tsunami waves, the residents had vanished without a trace, and others were cut off from any contact with the rest of the country. Reporter David Batty described the scene in Sendai for a *Guardian* article:

> *Miles from the ocean's edge, weary, mud-spattered survivors wandered streets strewn with fallen trees, crumpled cars, even small airplanes. Relics of lives now destroyed were everywhere—half a piano, a textbook, a soiled red sleeping bag. Rescue workers plied boats through murky waters around flooded structures, nosing their way through a sea of detritus, while smoke from at least one large fire billowed in the distance. Power and phone reception was cut, while*

hundreds of people lined up outside the few still-operating supermarkets for basic commodities. The gas stations on streets not covered with water were swamped with people waiting to fill their cars. . . .

The city's Wakabayashi district, which runs directly up to the sea, remained a swampy wasteland with murky, waist-high water. Most houses were completely flattened.[4]

As bad as the damage and destruction were in the tsunami-affected areas, another crisis loomed as a result of the earthquake and tsunami. A nuclear nightmare was unfolding due to the engulfing tsunami waters.

Many people who were homeless or forced to leave their homes stayed in crowded evacuation centers after the disasters.

The damaged Fukushima Daiichi nuclear power plant

A Nuclear Nightmare

*I*n addition to a huge earthquake and devastating tsunami waves, those who lived in the worst tsunami-damaged areas of Japan soon had another crisis to deal with. This one was more difficult to see, but it was potentially more deadly.

JAPAN'S POWER PLANTS

Japan has used nuclear energy since 1966 and relies on 54 nuclear reactors at 17 power plants to provide 30 percent of its electricity. Because Japan has few natural resources of its own to use for generating electricity, it has made nuclear power a priority. Japan uses the two standard methods for generating electricity: boiling water reactors (BWRs) and pressurized water reactors (PWRs). In both types of plants, high-pressure water passes around the nuclear reactor where it is heated. Then the water moves into a steam generator.

BWRs AND PWRs

These two types of nuclear plants differ in the way the cooling water is used and the way steam is produced. The BWR pumps water in a closed cycle. This means the water is reused again and again and never leaves the system. The water is heated by the

Other Japanese Plants

Eleven nuclear reactors closest to the epicenter, located at four separate nuclear power plants, were operating at the time of the earthquake. These included Fukushima Daiichi Reactor Number One, Reactor Number Two, and Reactor Number Three; Fukushima Daini Reactor Number One, Reactor Number Two, Reactor Number Three, and Reactor Number Four; Tohoku Electric Power Company's Reactor Number One, Reactor Number Two, and Reactor Number Three in Onagawa, and Japan Atomic Power Company's reactor in Tokai. They all automatically shut down as a result of the quake.

nuclear reaction as it moves around the fuel. When the water boils, the water and steam flow to the top of the reactor. At this point, they are separated and the steam is passed to the turbine generator, which uses the steam to turn the generator and create electricity. The steam then is condensed back into water and returned to the reactor.

The PWR system has two coolant loops, or piping systems, to transfer energy from the reactor to the turbine. The first loop contains water that is pumped

Chernobyl

Before the events at the Fukushima Daiichi plant in Japan, the worst nuclear accident in the world had occurred at Chernobyl in what was then the Soviet Union. On April 26, 1986, the Chernobyl nuclear power plant experienced an explosion and fire that caused a meltdown and exposed the nuclear reactor core. It sent large amounts of radioactivity into the atmosphere, some of which drifted into other countries in Europe. The accident was the result of a combination of operator human error, poor training, and bad plant design. Reports claim that only 31 people died as a direct result of the accident (many of them firefighters who were unwittingly exposed to high levels of radiation), but officials speculate that ultimately thousands will die as a result of radiation exposure that later leads to cancer.

The area around Chernobyl had to be abandoned and extensive environmental cleanup has been ongoing. The accident brought the world's focus on the Soviet nuclear power program and on the safety shortcuts and rushed plant construction that made the accident possible. Chernobyl is the only other nuclear accident in history—besides Fukushima—to have earned a 7 (the highest level) on the International Nuclear Events Scale.

through the nuclear core and then through a steam generator before looping around through the core again. A second loop of water is pumped through the other side of the steam generator, making the steam that goes to the turbine. The steam generator exchanges the heat from the first loop of water to the second loop. The steam in the second loop condenses back into water and is pumped back through the steam generator in a continuous cycle.

Japan's nuclear power plants were largely constructed using designs from US companies such as Westinghouse and General Electric. More important, the plants were designed to be located in a country that was prone to earthquakes and were planned to withstand earthquake damage. If ground movement above a certain severity was detected, the power plants would automatically shut down.

FUKUSHIMA DAIICHI AND DAINI

Two of Japan's nuclear plants, Fukushima Daiichi and Daini, are located approximately seven miles (11 km) apart on the coast of Japan, north of Tokyo. Both have BWRs and were designed by General Electric. These plants were designed to withstand tsunami waves up to 18.7 feet (5.7 m) in height.

A woman and her dog who live in the city of Koriyama, near Fukushima Daiichi, are scanned for radiation.

When the earthquake struck on March 11, the nuclear reactors at the two Fukushima power plants as well as two others in the area automatically shut down. Although the plants' other functions continued, the reactors stopped producing energy.

However, in the hour that followed the quake, the tsunami waves that came ashore near the two Fukushima plants were as high as 40 feet (12 m). Parts of Fukushima Daiichi were inundated with seawater.

The plants lost electric power, which also was something planned for in the design of the plant. At Fukushima Daiichi, emergency diesel generators kicked in automatically to provide the electric power for pumps and other components of the cooling system. But as the plant was flooded with water from the tsunami waves, the generators were engulfed and stopped working after an hour.

The tsunami water also swept away many of the plant's structures, including the system that brought in cooling water from the ocean. The turbine buildings were damaged. Meanwhile, the plant was forced to rely on power from batteries, which was depleted in approximately eight hours. Soon all of the emergency backup power was exhausted.

Cooling Spent Fuel

In addition to the plant damage, systems designed to cool the spent fuel failed. The spent fuel was stored in pools of water, but when the power was lost, the pumps were unable to maintain the water levels, which allowed the fuel to overheat. Without electricity to power its cooling systems, Fukushima Daiichi was now helpless and flooding damaged much of its facility. When the fuel inside a nuclear reactor is exposed and overheats, there is a real danger of a nuclear meltdown and the release of radioactivity into the environment.

EVACUATION

As news of the situation at Fukushima Daiichi spread, Japanese nuclear officials quickly reassured the public that there had been no release of radioactivity around the plant. But as the hours ticked past and the plant began running out of power for its cooling systems, Japan declared a state of emergency on March 12. The government ordered the evacuation of all residents within two miles (3 km) of the plant. The

Three Mile Island

The worst nuclear accident in the United States occurred on March 28, 1979, when the Three Mile Island nuclear power plant in Pennsylvania experienced a partial meltdown. As a result of operator error, insufficient training, and malfunctioning equipment, the TIM-2 reactor overheated, causing a partial meltdown and a small release of radioactivity. Pregnant women and young children were evacuated from the area as a precaution, but the extensive meltdown and contamination that were predicted never occurred.

order also advised those who lived within 6.2 miles (10 km) of the plant to remain indoors.

On March 15, the situation at Fukushima Daiichi escalated after a fire broke out in one of the reactors and an explosion occurred in the containment vessel of another. Unknown amounts of radiation had leaked into the atmosphere, and no one was sure if the containment vessel had been breached, exposing the reactor to the environment. Officials were now wondering if a severe nuclear meltdown was inevitable. One engineer commented in a report in the *New York Times*:

> "We are on the brink. We are now facing the worst-case scenario," said Hiroaki Koide, a senior reactor engineering specialist at the Research Reactor Institute of Kyoto University. "We can assume that the containment vessel at Reactor No. 2 is already breached. If there is heavy melting inside the reactor, large amounts of radiation will most definitely be released."[1]

Japan's nuclear industry faced a catastrophe that had already exceeded the severity of the Three Mile Island nuclear accident in the United States and might be approaching the level of the Chernobyl accident in the Soviet Union. Officials would have to figure out a way to keep the disaster at the plant from escalating—and they would have to do it fast.

A map of northern Japan shows the areas most affected by the earthquake.

Prime Minister Naoto Kan speaks at a press conference on March 25, 2011.

AN ESCALATING CRISIS

The situation at the Fukushima nuclear plant steadily worsened. Elsewhere, survivors struggled to find shelter, food, and water while rescue teams searched for the living and dealt with the dead. As Japan's Prime Minister Naoto Kan said in a press conference, "I think that the earthquake, tsunami, and the situation at our nuclear reactors makes up the worst crisis in the 65 years since [World War II]."[1]

Heating Up

At Fukushima Daiichi, six separate reactors were within the plant, and three had overheated once the cooling system lost power. In addition, the spent fuel pools also lost water and were overheating. In addition to disabling the plant's generators, seawater flooding had disabled the system of heat exchangers that took heat from the reactors and dumped it into the ocean.

As the reactors continued to heat up, the pressure inside their containment vessels also increased. This resulted in some venting of radioactive materials to other parts of the plant and ultimately into the environment. The pressure caused a hydrogen explosion on March 13

Futaba

Four years before the earthquake in Japan, town officials in Futaba were in favor of a plan to expand the Fukushima nuclear plant two miles (3 km) from their town. It would provide more jobs for the town. After the earthquake, the town's entire population of 6,900 had to be evacuated and have been moved from shelter to shelter as the town's mayor attempts to keep them all together. "The important thing is that we stay together as one," Mayor Idogawa said. "It helps us help you. It helps us make sure everybody is all right."[2]

when hydrogen mixed with air and ignited, blowing off much of the roof and protective cladding on the top part of the building.

Plant officials feared a total meltdown of the nuclear reactor where the fuel would melt and possibly destroy the plant building. It would also release huge amounts of radioactivity into the environment. The only option was for the workers to keep flooding the reactors with seawater in an attempt to cool them. This created radioactive steam, which leaked from the plant and could continue to do so for weeks or even months. The struggle to cope with overheated reactors and spent fuel pools continued for weeks and often required heroic measures from the plant's workers:

> This was undertaken by hundreds of Tepco [the company that owned the nuclear plant] employees as well as some contractors, supported by firefighting and military personnel. Some of the Tepco staff had lost homes, and even families, in the tsunami, and were living in temporary accommodation under great difficulties and privation, with some personal risk.[3]

Workers struggled to control the badly damaged plant to prevent a radioactive catastrophe. By the

afternoon of March 15, their hard
work seemed to be making progress
as radiation levels stabilized and
then declined. Then radiation levels
increased after a new explosion and
fire in Reactor Number Four on
March 16. The reactor had been shut
down before the earthquake, but it
still had spent fuel pools that were
overheating.

Radiological Material

On March 16, authorities
announced that Reactor Number Two
at Fukushima might have ruptured
and seemed to be sending radioactive
steam into the environment.
In addition to this break, it was
discovered that the containment
vessel in Reactor Number Two had
also cracked.

The situation in Japan prompted
the United Nations to issue a forecast
of the possible movement of the
plume of radioactivity that was now in

The International Nuclear and Radiological Event Scale

The International Nuclear and Radiological Event Scale (INES) is a tool for letting the public know the severity and danger of a particular nuclear event. It can be used for events at nuclear power plants and in anything involving the transportation, storage, and use of radioactive materials. The scale ranges from Level 1 to Level 7. The higher the number, the more severe the nuclear event was. Levels 1 through 3 are considered a nuclear incident. Levels 4 through 7 indicate a nuclear accident. At first, the events at Fukushima Daiichi were rated as a Level 5, but later raised to a 7, the highest level and one indicating a major accident.

the atmosphere and traveling across the Pacific. The forecast was not released to the general public, but the *New York Times* obtained information about its projected path:

> *The Japan forecast shows that the radioactive plume will probably miss the agency's monitoring stations at Midway and in the Hawaiian Islands but is likely to be detected in the Aleutians and at a monitoring station in Sacramento. The forecast assumes that radioactivity in Japan is released continuously and forms a rising plume. It ends with the plume heading into Southern California and the American Southwest, including Nevada, Utah, and Arizona.* [4]

Just a few days after the earthquake, the US Navy's Seventh Fleet was stationed approximately 100 miles (161 km) off the coast of Japan. The fleet detected low amounts of radioactivity in the atmosphere. However, Gregory Jaczko, the head

The Nuclear Regulatory Commission

The Nuclear Regulatory Commission (NRC) is an agency created in 1974 by the US Congress. According to the NRC Web site, its purpose is "to enable the nation to safely use radioactive materials for beneficial civilian purposes while ensuring that people and the environment are protected. The NRC regulates commercial nuclear power plants and other uses of nuclear materials, such as in nuclear medicine, through licensing, inspection and enforcement of its requirements." [5]

of the Nuclear Regulatory Commission (NRC), reassured the public at a press conference at the White House:

> *You just aren't going to have any radiological material that, by the time it traveled those large distances, could present any risk to the American public. Based on the design and the distances involved, it is very unlikely that there would be any harmful impacts.*[6]

DESPERATE MEASURES

Meanwhile, the need to cool the Fukushima reactors as quickly as possible led to some unconventional methods. The spent fuel pool water was replenished by adding seawater through gaps in the roof and protective cladding. However, the spent fuel pool in Reactor Number Four appeared to have damage to its sides or floor, making it difficult to refill it with water. Helicopters and water cannons were used to spray water on the reactors, but the high levels of radiation made it difficult to approach the reactor closely enough to make the water effective. Officials concentrated on Reactor Number Three, which used a special kind of fuel known as MOX or mixed oxide. MOX is made in part from reclaimed plutonium and would create a more dangerous radioactive plume if it was released.

On March 16, the escalating events at the nuclear plants prompted Japan's Nuclear Safety Commission to ask everyone under the age of 40 evacuating the danger zone to take doses of iodine. This was especially important because products such as milk could be contaminated by radiation after dairy cows ingested tainted grass. Infants and children were particularly vulnerable. As

Iodine

When there is a possibility of radioactive contamination, people may be advised to take iodine tablets. There are two types of iodine: radioactive Iodine-131 and Potassium Iodide. Iodine-131 is a byproduct of the nuclear fission reaction that creates nuclear energy. Potassium Iodide is a stable form of iodine that the body requires in order to make thyroid hormones and comes as tablets or liquid.

The thyroid absorbs both of these types of iodine and does not know the difference between the two. When there is the threat that a body might absorb radioactive Iodine-131, taking stable iodine tablets fills up the thyroid until it is full and cannot absorb any more. This helps keep the radioactive iodine from being absorbed.

However, iodine tablets only protect the thyroid and no other parts of the body. Its effectiveness also depends on how much time has elapsed since the body's exposure to radioactive iodine, how fast the nonradioactive iodine can be absorbed into the bloodstream, and how much radioactive iodine the person was exposed to. Those who are most vulnerable to radioactive iodine include unborn babies, infants, and children up to the age of 18, and people with thyroid problems. Adults over 40 years old have the lowest risk.

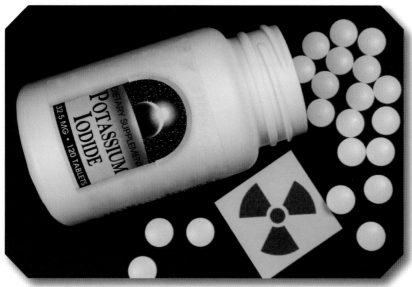

Iodine tablets can help a person's body from absorbing radioactive iodine.

many as 80,000 residents left the area, and the government estimated that they would not be able to return home for at least six months.

By March 22, workers at Fukushima Daiichi had managed to reconnect power cables to all six reactors, restringing electricity to power cooling systems. They found that some of the machinery, including water pumps, had been damaged and was in need of repair. The next day, radioactive iodine was found in Tokyo's water system, leading to panic and a warning not to let infants drink it. With the

Cesium 137

On March 31, 2011, a long-lasting radioactive element known as Cesium 137, another product of nuclear fission, was detected 25 miles (40 km) from Fukushima Daiichi. The level of Cesium 137 was high enough to create a long-term danger, prompting many people to question whether the evacuation zone for the plant should be expanded. A few days later, it was also found in the plumes of steam being released by the nuclear plant.

rush to buy bottled water at Tokyo stores, the government considered importing bottled water from overseas.

The crisis at Fukushima Daiichi inched toward the point where officials could finally control the crippled power plant, but it was a slow process. By March 25, officials quietly encouraged a voluntary evacuation within a radius of 12.42 to 18.64 miles (20 to 30 km) of the plant. As radioactive plumes of smoke and steam billowed into the air, and contamination was found in the soil near the plant, it was clear the nuclear nightmare would not be easily resolved.

*A person believed to be exposed to radiation is evacuated
from the Fukushima plant.*

Children at Nobiru Elementary School wave good-bye to Danish Crown Prince Frederick during his visit to Japan. Many celebrities and foreign diplomats came to see the tsunami devastation and help finance relief.

THE WORLD RESPONDS

ecause news coverage is so instantaneous, many people around the world watched in horror as the tsunami waves engulfed the coast of Japan just an hour after the quake. And as quickly as the devastation occurred, offers of aid poured in from all over the world. Just three days after the quake, 91 countries and international organizations had offered to assist with relief efforts.

Help from Everyone

Even countries that had recently suffered disasters, such as Pakistan and Bolivia, offered support. Some were willing to send money while others sent more tangible relief, such as food, water, and other supplies. Medical personnel, search and rescue teams with dogs, and nuclear experts offered their time and expertise. Sri Lanka, which had suffered from a devastating tsunami in 2004, sent $1 million in aid as well as a military and medical relief team. Great Britain sent a fire brigade of search and rescue experts along with heavy lifting and cutting equipment and two dogs. The United States sent military equipment, including ships, airplanes, and helicopters. The United States also allocated $35 million in relief funds to Operation Tomodachi. In Japanese, *tomodachi* means "friendship."

Traveling Radiation

By March 28, many utility companies in the United States, which are equipped to monitor for radiation in the atmosphere, reported finding trace amounts of radiation from the Japan nuclear plants. Utilities in South Carolina, Florida, Massachusetts, Nevada, and several Western states reported trace amounts of Iodine-131. This small amount was not harmful to public health.

Rescue Dogs

The search and rescue dogs sent to help in Japan are special dogs. Not only are they trained to find people in the midst of wreckage, but they can also tell—by scent—the difference between living people and dead bodies. This helps rescuers to prioritize as they look first for those who might still be alive. Some of the best rescue dogs are German shepherds, Belgian sheepdogs, golden retrievers, and Labrador retrievers.

Countries, whether large or small, gave generously to help the people of Japan. Even China, which has historically been a rival of Japan, offered assistance.

International organizations helped as well. The group *Medecins Sans Frontieres* (Doctors Without Borders) sent a team of ten people to operate clinics in Miyagi Prefecture. The United Nations Telecommunications Agency sent emergency telephone equipment, including satellite phones equipped with GPS, to help teams that searched for missing people. The World Bank offered its support as well. Robert Zoellick, World Bank president, said:

This is a heartbreaking situation and the World Bank Group stands ready to help the government and the people of Japan in the recovery efforts. As the extent of the tragic loss of life and damage is still unfolding in Japan we are also monitoring potential impacts in countries across the region and are ready to offer our support. [1]

US soldier volunteers bring bottles of water to victims at a shelter in the city of Rikuzentakata in northern Japan.

On the Ground

The rescue efforts were often poignant and difficult for those involved. David Darg, a rescue worker with the Operation Blessing group, blogged about his experiences in one of the areas hardest hit by the earthquake and tsunami:

> *The leadership at the shelter was so grateful when we told them we had rice. They are feeding the 1,000 people in the shelter and 200 locals who are without food. . . . Up till now*

the center had only been able to provide bread in very limited amounts and this was difficult especially for the elderly who have been used to eating rice three times a day for their whole lives and who were very hungry. [2]

While much of the aid was focused on the survivors of the earthquake and tsunami, especially those whose homes had been destroyed, other aid focused on the dangerous situation at the nuclear power plants.

EXPERT HELP

The NRC immediately sent assistance to Japan on March 12. Two of the NRC's members were experts on BWRs and joined a disaster response team. "We have some of the most expert people in this field in the world working for the NRC and we stand ready to assist in any way possible," said NRC Chairman Gregory Jaczko. [3] The NRC also opened an emergency operations center, staffed 24 hours a day, at its Maryland office to deal with the disaster. The operations center was designed to assist the Japanese government and to protect the safety of the American people in the event of contamination reaching the United States from Japan. The NRC also posted extensive questions and answers on its Web site for further information about the accident and to quell fears about a similar event occurring in the United States.

Other countries also offered the help of their nuclear efforts. Canada sent a Disaster Victim Identification team made up of chemical, biological, radiological, and nuclear technical experts. Russia said that its state nuclear corporation, Rosatom, would be available to help with problems at the nuclear plants. US Navy ships were deployed offshore

Spokane's Milk

On March 30, 2011, the *Seattle Times* newspaper reported that federal regulators had found a small amount of Iodine-131 in samples of milk from Spokane, Washington. This was the first time any trace of radiation from Japan had been found in US food. Milk was monitored because it is one of the most common ways for humans to ingest Iodine-131, since it falls with rain, gets deposited on vegetation, and then is eaten by milk-producing cows. According to the article:

Health experts said consumers need not worry. The sample, taken March 25, remained 5,000 times below levels of concern set by the Food and Drug Administration (FDA), even for infants. In fact, the amount of radiation in the sample was tens of thousands of times lower than what one might be exposed to during a round-trip cross-country flight, said Patricia Hansen, a senior scientist with the FDA. In addition, Iodine 131 also has a short half-life—about eight days—so health officials expect radiation levels to drop off quickly. "The amount we're talking about is minuscule," said Mary Selecky, secretary of the Washington Department of Health.[4]

to scan for radiation levels in the atmosphere. On March 18, a Massachusetts company, called iRobot, sent four of its specialized robots to aid Japan. Two were "pack-bots" used by the military and the police to maneuver in dangerous areas and detect toxic chemicals or radiation in the air. The other two were "warrior" robots that can lift and tow heavy objects. Tim Trainer of iRobot said,

> *The ideal thing about a robot is we can send it off into the hazardous zone or that unknown zone while keeping the operator safe in some standoff position.*[5]

But despite all the aid pouring in from around the world, the situation in Japan was still grim, and nowhere was it worse than at the stricken nuclear plants. As aftershocks continued to shake the country, some of them as strong as regular earthquakes, Japan knew the worst was far from over.

A robot developed at the Japanese Chiba Institute of Technology's Future
Robotics Technology Center was sent to Fukushima.

Children living near Fukushima were given dosimeters to help monitor their exposure to radiation.

CONTAMINATION

Even though some aspects of the crisis at Fukushima Daiichi seemed to be resolving, officials had ordered additional evacuations by March 25. Those people who had been told to remain indoors before were now told to leave their homes. The plant's crisis had suffered a setback when it found that some of the workers had received unexpectedly high doses of radiation. It was feared that the reactor vessel of Reactor Number Three had been breached. This reactor ran on MOX fuel, and the danger of contamination for people outside the plant was now more serious.

DANGEROUS SIDE EFFECTS

Because of the efforts of the workers to cool the fuel inside the reactors, some dangerous side effects had developed in the area surrounding the plant. On March 28, the *New York Times* reported that contaminated water was escaping from the damaged plant and would soon leak into the ocean. The report stated:

> Tokyo Electric Power Company, which runs the Fukushima Daiichi Nuclear Power station, said late Monday that it had

Measuring Radiation

Radiation exposure is measured in different ways. In the United States, the measurements used are rems and millirems (mrem). One thousand mrem make up one rem. Japan uses units called Sieverts (Sv) and milliSieverts (mSv) to measure radiation. One thousand mSv make up one Sv. One Sv is equal to 100 rems. One mSv then equals 100 mrem. The average person in the United States receives approximately 360 mrem, or 3.6 mSv, per year from naturally occurring background radiation and from X-rays.

detected higher levels of plutonium in soil samples taken from within the compound a week ago, raising fears of yet another dangerous element that may be escaping the crippled reactors. . . . The nuclear safety agency also reported that radioactive iodine 131 was detected Sunday at a concentration 1,150 times the maximum allowable level in a seawater sample taken about a mile north of the drainage outlets of reactor units 1 through 4. It also said that the amount of cesium 137 found in water about 1,000 feet [305 m] from the plant was 20 times the normal level.[1]

Some of the contamination had escaped from the

Don't Eat That

On March 20, Japan placed restrictions on food that had been produced in two prefectures near the Fukushima nuclear plant. High levels of radioactive cesium and iodine were detected in spinach and milk. Shiitake mushrooms were later added to the list of banned produce. The levels of iodine found in milk from the area around Fukushima ranged from 20 percent over the acceptable limit to more than 17 times the acceptable limit. Spinach grown in a neighboring prefecture was found to have levels of iodine as much as 27 times the acceptable limit.

Experts said that someone who ate the contaminated food would only receive the same amount of radiation that they would receive from one CT scan. Of bigger concern was the effect that it would have on farmers, who relied on selling produce in order to survive. A security expert from MIT, Jim Walsh, commented in a CNN news story,

The government is going to have to grapple with what to do about that. If they outlaw all the produce from that region, that pretty much is putting the stamp of death on those farmers. They're never going to be able to sell any produce.[2]

reactors as a result of the efforts being made to cool the fuel. As workers pumped more water into the reactors, it was overflowing and escaping the plant through overflow tunnels. Several workers were burned when they stepped into radioactive water inside the turbine building of Reactor Number Three. Another worker, wearing higher boots, was not injured. Even after the high radiation levels were discovered, no workers were evacuated.

Tokyo Electric Power Company (TEPCO) reported that 19 workers had been exposed to radiation levels of 100 millisieverts (mSv), a unit used for measuring doses of radiation. A dose of 100 mSv would make a human more likely to develop cancer. If a worker received more than 250 mSv, he or she would no longer be allowed to work in a nuclear power plant, having received the maximum allowable dosage of radiation. As the radiation levels rose inside the Fukushima reactors, TEPCO was forced to hire more workers. According to an article on Bloomberg.com:

> *The utility increased its workforce at the Fukushima Dai-Ichi plant to 322 yesterday from 180 on March 16 as it tried to douse water over spent nuclear fuel rods to prevent them*

melting and leaking lethal radiation. Levels beside exposed rods would deliver a fatal dose in 16 seconds, said David Lochbaum, a nuclear physicist for the Union of Concerned Scientists and a former U.S. Nuclear Regulatory Commission safety instructor. The permissible cumulative radiation exposure was more than doubled three days ago to extend the time nuclear workers could legally spend onsite. Radiation was measured at 20 millisieverts per hour near the site's administration building, Hikaru Kuroda, the utility's maintenance chief, told reporters today. An hour's exposure there would equate to the most workers are typically allowed in one year, frustrating efforts to cool nuclear fuel.[3]

Hamaoka

On May 9, 2011, another Japanese nuclear power plant shut down, even though it was not damaged by the quake. The Hamaoka power plant is located approximately 125 miles (201 km) south of Tokyo, in the same type of seismic area as Fukushima. It was built near a fault line in a geologically unstable location. The government requested that the plant shut down until it had an emergency plan in the event of another earthquake and tsunami.

TELLING THE TRUTH

By April 6, 2011, the US NRC reported that some of the core from one of Fukushima Daiichi's reactors had most likely leaked from the reactor's steel containment vessel into the bottom of the containment structure. This indicated that the damage to the plant was probably much worse than initially thought. By April 12, Japan raised its assessment of the accident from a 5 to a 7 on the INES. Officials felt that Fukushima Daiichi's leaking radiation levels could eventually be greater than those released by the Chernobyl disaster in 1986.

There were political implications as well. Prime Minister Kan was criticized for his handling of the nuclear crisis. One of his advisers, Toshiso Kosako, resigned. He said the government had failed to follow the law and the Japanese population had not been protected well enough from radiation. According to the *New York Times*:

> *Kosako had pointed to a recent government decision allowing children living near the crippled nuclear plant to receive doses of radiation equal to the international standard for [nuclear] plant workers—a level higher than those set for the public.*[4]

Around the world, officials and nuclear experts chimed in. They argued that inconsistent regulations and rules that were not enforced or did not exist made Japan's nuclear plants unnecessarily vulnerable to a disaster.

Bad News Keeps Coming

Many people wondered why the news from Fukushima kept changing and getting worse. According to an article in *Time* magazine, "The utility says it is only starting to understand what it's dealing with. The problem with a nuclear accident is that the damage gets done early, and fast. Even after the makeshift cooling system started to work, TEPCO knew there was damage to the fuel inside the reactors, but . . . it wasn't until radiation inside the reactor buildings dropped to safe enough levels for workers to go in and take measurements that the company could start to ascertain the problem. . . . 'The situation will gradually be getting better,' says Dr. Bing Luk. 'As long as they keep the system cool, then it will just stay as is. In a few years, maybe they can start thinking about retrieving some of the fuel rods.'"[5]

Clearly, it was going to take a considerable amount of time and money to bring the Fukushima Daiichi plant to a point known as "cold shutdown," when it would be stable. Officials estimated it could take at least nine months. Many people considered this to be an optimistic estimate, especially after a pair of robots sent into the reactor buildings came back with radiation levels that were too high for workers to venture inside even for a short period of time.

By May 5, workers were able to enter the damaged reactor buildings, hoping to install a ventilator that would help lower radiation levels. Just days later, after previously saying that Japan was still committed to nuclear energy, the *New York Times* reported:

> *In a sharp reversal, Prime Minister Naoto Kan said Japan would abandon plans to*

Farmers from communities near Fukushima place spinach in front of TEPCO and demand to be compensated by the government for the produce they cannot sell due to contamination fears.

build new nuclear reactors, saying his country needed to "start from scratch" in creating a new energy policy. Mr. Kan said Japan would retain nuclear and fossil fuels as energy sources, but vowed to add two new pillars to Japan's energy policy: renewable energy and conservation.[6]

By May 23, TEPCO finally acknowledged the severity of the accident at Fukushima Daiichi. According to the *New York Times*:

Help Us Now

On April 13, 2011, residents who had been forced from their homes because of the Fukushima nuclear plant accident protested outside the office of TEPCO, which owned the nuclear plant. Residents demanded compensation for the fact that they had no homes and no jobs. Seventy-three-year-old Shigeaki Konno was an auto repair mechanic. He was evacuated from his home just seven miles (11 km) from the Fukushima Daiichi nuclear plant. He said, "I can't work and that means I have no money."[8] Company officials bowed in apology and pledged to provide cash payments.

In a belated acknowledgment of the severity of Japan's nuclear disaster, the Tokyo Electric Power Company said that three of the stricken Fukushima plant's reactors likely suffered fuel meltdowns in the early days of the crisis. The plant's operator also said that it was possible that the pressure vessels in the three stricken reactors, which house the uranium fuel rods, had been breached as well, but that most of the fuel remained inside the vessels.[7]

The health and safety of many people in the area surrounding the Fukushima plant had been compromised. Many had left their homes, unsure if they would ever be able to return. Others, particularly farmers, faced a future in which they were unable to sell their produce because of possible contamination. And yet this was just one aspect of the long-term effects the earthquake and tsunami disaster would have on Japan.

Thousands of people protested in Tokyo on May 7, 2011, against the use of nuclear power.

On June 24, 2011, the first swimming beach in the eastern region of Japan affected by the disasters reopened.

Aftermath

As of April 25, 2011, the official death toll for the disaster was increased to 14,133, and more than 13,346 were listed as missing. It was expected that the death toll could surpass 20,000. Of those who survived, more than 130,000 were living in temporary shelters because their homes had been destroyed or they had been forced to evacuate.

An Uneasy Peace

On May 18, 2011, the International Atomic Energy Agency (IAEA) issued a status report for the four Fukushima reactors. A cover was being constructed for Reactor Number One as an additional measure to keep any radioactive substances from escaping. This was intended to be an emergency measure until more long-term measures could be taken, such as advanced radiation shielding. Fukushima's owner, TEPCO, reported that the damage to the reactor was worse than previously thought and had occurred much earlier in the disaster. However, because of continuing efforts to cool the reactor with water, it was

Indonesia and Nuclear Power

Indonesia is located in the Pacific Ring of Fire and also is prone to earthquakes and tsunamis. But even though Indonesia witnessed the effects of the March 11 earthquake on Japan's nuclear plants, Indonesia is conducting a study aimed at bringing nuclear power to its country. The three-year study is expected to lead to the construction of a nuclear plant. However, many Indonesians are reluctant to see nuclear power in their country after the situation in Japan.

unlikely that any large amounts of radiation would be released in the future. Freshwater continued to be injected into Reactor Number One, Reactor Number Two, and Reactor Number Three. Their temperatures and pressures remained stable.

The spent fuel pool in Reactor Number Four was being reinforced while still receiving the necessary water to keep the fuel cool. Officials also minimized the amount of water leaving the plants and entering the ocean. They used an anti-scattering agent by spraying a chemical onto the area around the plant to prevent any radioactive materials in dust from becoming airborne and being carried further away from the plant. According to *World Nuclear News*:

> *In the long accident sequence at the power plant since the tsunami of 11 March there has been venting of radioactive steam and the apparent rupture of unit 2's torus [a doughnut-shaped ring of water located below the reactor vessel, which could also vent radioactive steam] as well as various fires near used fuel ponds and hydrogen explosions. All of these have served to distribute [radioactive substances], much of which landed in the immediate area of the site on muddy ground left by the tsunami.*[1]

Officials continued to monitor the air and soil in 47 prefectures surrounding the plant as well as to test food and milk samples from 15 prefectures. By May 18, the only food restrictions still in place were in Fukushima Prefecture and included certain types of fish, raw milk, turnips, bamboo shoots, mushrooms, spinach, and cabbage.

Ultimately, once the plant reaches cold shutdown and is safely decommissioned, the entire facility and all of its reactors will be shut down. On April 17, TEPCO released its

Decommissioning

Decommissioning is the process of taking a nuclear power plant out of service. The NRC designates three types of decommissioning as DECON, SAFESTOR, and ENTOMB. DECON requires taking a plant down immediately and removing any radioactive materials. SAFESTOR is similar, except that the plant is allowed to sit long enough for some radioactivity to decay, which usually takes years. ENTOMB involves encasing any radioactive elements in concrete and monitoring them until the radioactivity level decreases.

The Chernobyl Nuclear Power Plant, in what was once the Soviet Union, has been decommissioned using the ENTOMB method, which encased the entire damaged reactor in concrete. The Three Mile Island plant in the United States was decommissioned using the SAFESTOR approach. The radioactive fuel was removed from the plant, but the building was left to decay. Most likely, Fukushima Daiichi will be decommissioned using the DECON or SAFESTOR method since officials have already determined that they would not be using the ENTOMB method. Estimates suggest it could take 30 years to fully dismantle the plant and its reactors.

plan, which is referred to as a road map, for shutting down the plant safely over a period of nine months:

> *The plan is divided into two stages. In the first three months, cooling systems would be installed to lower temperatures in reactors and radiation levels in the region. In the second six-month phase, the plant would be cleared of wreckage and contaminated water and encased in a covering, including an air filter to prevent any further radiation being released into the atmosphere.*[2]

Many nuclear experts consider this plan to be too optimistic. It could take many years to reach this point, and perhaps even longer, before all traces of radiation were gone.

By June 2011, the situation at the plant was still serious. Workers were still using water to cool the reactors, but once the water was run through a reactor it would be contaminated with radioactivity. Running out of places to store the contaminated cooling water, the plant quickly built a filtration system for the water. Officials at the plant hoped they could filter the water and reuse it to cool the reactors. However, the filtration system broke down on June 18 after only five hours of operation. No one knows when it will be safe for residents of the area to return to their homes and if the farmers will ever be able to market their produce again.

An Economic Disaster

Japan's economy also became a long-term victim of the earthquake and tsunami. The economy was severely weakened by the disaster. In addition to the tremendous costs involved in caring for survivors, cleaning up, and rebuilding, many factories were forced to shut down. This not only affects those who work in the factories but also Japan's economy as a whole. Japan relies heavily on exporting goods to other countries. Immediately after the earthquake, companies such as Toyota and Nissan closed factories, as did companies such as Nestle and Sony.

The Japanese stock market also suffered as a result of the disaster and the crisis at its nuclear plants. Japan

New Safety Possibilities

A construction company in Toyoda in the Aichi Prefecture of Japan has invented a bright orange pod-like structure that could protect people in the event of another tsunami. The steel pods, which come in several sizes to hold from four to 25 people, include seat belts, helmets, and infant seats. They are primarily designed for the elderly and very young children who have the most trouble outrunning incoming tsunami waves. The pod will keep them safe as it is carried by the wave and is designed to reach the surface in just 20 seconds.

A memorial was held at an elementary school in the city of Ishinomaki in Miyagi Prefecture, where 74 of 108 students died in the tsunami.

had only just started to recover from an economic recession at the time of the earthquake. After the earthquake, investors around the world were nervous about the situation in Japan and especially its nuclear situation, which made them reluctant to invest in Japanese companies. Most likely, the country will struggle economically until it has rebuilt its infrastructure (utilities, water, roads, and buildings) and factories can resume manufacturing and exporting goods.

THE TOUGHEST RECOVERY

By July 2011, the official death and missing persons count from the disaster had risen to more than 22,000 people. Tens of thousands of people were still living in shelters. Many still did not know when or if they could ever return home.

Many people who survived the disaster were suffering from post-traumatic stress disorder and other psychological trauma. The stress of fleeing for one's life and losing families and homes often brings on symptoms such as insomnia and anxiety. These symptoms can occur immediately after the disaster or after time has passed. The stress of not knowing whether family members are alive or dead can heighten these mental issues. According to Melissa Brymer, a clinical psychologist, who was consulted for an article in the *Los Angeles Times:*

> There will be people who will be able to move back to how things were, and there's going to be a subset of people who are going to have more mental health issues. [3]

Anyone can suffer from mental health problems after a tragic experience, such as living through an earthquake and tsunami. People are at a greater risk for developing psychological problems if they have had one in the past or been in a similar disaster before. Brymer suspected that children who were separated from their families or orphaned during the disasters were also at a higher risk. Counseling was being offered for many victims of the tragedy. Brymer noted that supportive communities can help people struggling after a disaster, "[H]ow the community supports itself can be a mediating factor in how people deal with a disaster."[4]

The Japanese Red Cross said that one in ten of the survivors of the disaster might now be suffering from post-traumatic stress disorder. This could amount to tens of thousands of people and may be the

A Dog Hero

One of the most poignant images from the Japanese disaster was of a dog, not a human. A video captured a tired, unkempt dog standing guard over another injured dog. The dog refused to leave his companion and occasionally stroked it with a paw. It took rescuers an hour before the guard dog allowed the rescuers to take his injured friend to a clinic.

longest-lasting legacy of March 11, 2011. Teacher Yukiko Horie, who lost several of her students in the tsunami, talked about one girl who survived. "[She] remembers the terrible things and cannot sleep. . . . I don't know how to help her. I think the terrible experience will stay with the girls for the rest of their lives."[5] Horie also suffers from the incident.

Looking to the Future

The Japanese people know they will survive this disaster, just as they survived other natural disasters and wars. Many know they survived because of the earthquake and tsunami warning systems set up by the government and because their society is trained to listen and act on those warnings immediately. The Japanese people will pull together and do what they need to do to recover with continued help from their world neighbors. Even the youngest members of Japanese society know this is the time to look beyond themselves. According to an article in *Time* magazine:

> *Even those who never lived through Japan's last days of privation during World War II know what is required of them as Japanese citizens. "We, the young generation, will*

The Women's World Cup

In July 2011, while people in Japan still mourned those lost in the disasters, they experienced a rare moment of celebration. Japan's women's soccer team made a surprise run in the Women's World Cup. On July 17, the team upset the favored US team in a dramatic final. Japan came from behind twice before eventually winning in a penalty shoot-out. It was the first time an Asian country had won the cup. After the game, the team thanked people around the world for supporting Japan during the tragedy. The players hoped their win would inspire their country.

unite and work hard to get over this tragedy," says Mamiko Shimizu, a 24-year-old graduate student. "It's now our time to rebuild Japan."[6]

Survivors mourn the dead.

TIMELINE

1923	1968	1995
An earthquake in the Tokyo region of Japan kills more than 100,000 people.	The Pacific Tsunami Warning Center is established.	On January 17, an earthquake hits central Japan and the city of Kobe, killing thousands and causing widespread damage.

2011	2011	2011
Prime Minister Naoto Kan declares a "nuclear emergency status" at the Fukushima plant at 7:30 p.m. on March 12.	On March 12 at 10:00 p.m., officials begin evacuating residents within 2 miles (3 km) of the Fukushima plant.	On March 13, a hydrogen explosion occurs at Fukushima.

2007	2011	2011
Japan launches an online early warning system for earthquakes and tsunamis.	At approximately 2:46 p.m. on March 11, an earthquake strikes Japan. It is followed an hour later by a tsunami.	At 3:45 p.m. on March 11, officials at the Fukushima Daiichi plant report that emergency generators for three of its reactors have failed.

2011	2011	2011
On March 13, Fukushima plant workers struggle to cool the nuclear reactors.	In the afternoon of March 15, radiation levels decrease at Fukushima.	On March 16, radiation levels increase and there is a fire and explosion in Reactor Number Four.

TIMELINE

2011

Radioactive steam is released from the Fukushima plant on March 16.

2011

On March 22, workers reconnect power cables to all six reactors.

2011

On March 23, radioactive iodine is found in Tokyo's water supply. The government warns that infants should not drink the water.

2011

On April 6, the US NRC reports that the damage at Fukushima was much worse than initially believed.

2011

On April 12, the INES rating for the disaster at Fukushima is raised from 5 to 7.

2011

TEPCO announces on April 17 a 9-month plan for safely shutting down the Fukushima plant.

2011

2011

2011

Officials encourage evacuation from an even larger area around the Fukushima plant on March 25.

Contaminated water leaks from the Fukushima plant and flows into the ocean on March 28.

Radioactive Cesium 137 is found in soil 25 miles (40 km) from the Fukushima plant on March 31.

2011

2011

2011

On May 9, Prime Minister Kan announces Japan will abandon plans for new nuclear power plants.

On May 23, TEPCO admits that in the first days of the crisis, all three reactors at the Fukushima plant suffered meltdowns.

On June 18, a filtration system meant to filter radioactive cooling water at the plant breaks down after five hours.

Essential Facts

Date of Event

March 11, 2011

Place of Event

Japan, especially the northeast coast and the Fukushima Daiichi nuclear power plant

Key Players

* The Japanese people
* Fukushima plant workers
* Prime Minister Naoto Kan
* Tokyo Electronic Power Company

Highlights of Event

❖ An earthquake rated at 9.0 on the Richter scale struck Japan on March 11, 2011.

❖ The March 11 earthquake caused a devastating tsunami less than an hour later, strongly affecting Japan's northeast coast.

❖ The Fukushima Daiichi nuclear plant was damaged in the earthquake and tsunami and experienced meltdowns in three of its reactors, releasing radioactivity into the surrounding area.

❖ On May 9, Prime Minister Kan announced that Japan would abandon plans for new nuclear power plants.

Quote

"I think that the earthquake, tsunami and the situation at our nuclear reactors makes up the worst crisis in the 65 years since [World War II]."—*Prime Minister Naoto Kan*

GLOSSARY

aftershock
A small earthquake or tremor that follows a major earthquake.

concentric
Circles or rings having a common center.

contamination
The presence of unwanted radioactive materials on surfaces, structures, objects, or in water.

core
The part of a nuclear reactor that contains nuclear fuel.

detritus
Disintegrated materials or debris.

epicenter
A point directly above the center or disturbance from which the shock waves of an earthquake radiate.

meltdown
When a nuclear reactor overheats, melting its fuel rods and causing the release of radioactive materials and radiation.

nuclear
A form of energy that comes from particles found in atoms.

nuclear reactor
A piece of equipment where a nuclear reaction can be started, maintained, and controlled, generating energy.

plume
A visible pattern of smoke emitted from a stack, flue, or chimney.

prefecture
An official Japanese territory, similar to a state in the United States.

radioactivity
Radiation emitted by a nuclear reaction.

receding
Moving away, retreating, withdrawing.

seismic
> Relating to or caused by an earthquake or vibration of the earth due to natural or artificial causes.

shielding
> A protective barrier against nuclear radiation, such as a lead or concrete barrier around a reactor.

spent fuel
> Nuclear fuel that has been removed from a nuclear reactor once it has been depleted and can no longer be used to create nuclear fission.

turbine
> A machine with blades driven by steam that produces electricity.

waterline
> The line on a beach or coast that is reached by the water of an ocean or lake.

ADDITIONAL RESOURCES

SELECTED BIBLIOGRAPHY

Atkins, Stephen E. *Historical Encyclopedia of Atomic Energy*. Westport, CT: Greenwood, 2000. Print.

Christine Gibson. *Smithsonian Extreme Natural Disasters*. New York: HarperCollins, 2007. Print

Medvedev, Zhores. *The Legacy of Chernobyl*. New York: Norton, 1990. Print.

Tibballs, Geoff. *Tsunami: The World's Most Terrifying Natural Disaster*. London: Carlton, 2005. Print.

FURTHER READINGS

Levy, Matthys, and Mario Salvadori. *Earthquakes, Volcanoes, and Tsunamis: Projects and Principles for Beginning Geologists*. Chicago: Chicago Review, 2009. Print.

Lusted, Marcia Amidon, and Greg Lusted. *Building History: A Nuclear Power Plant*. Farmington Hills, MI: Lucent, 2005. Print.

Stewart, Melissa. *Inside Earthquakes*. New York; Sterling, 2011. Print.

Web Links

To learn more about the 2011 Japan disasters, visit ABDO Publishing Company online at **www.abdopublishing.com**. Web sites about the 2011 Japan disasters are featured on our Book Links page. These links are routinely monitored and updated to provide the most current information available.

Places to Visit

Kobe Earthquake Memorial Museum
Kobe, Japan
http://www.dri.ne.jp/english/index.html
This museum provides information about earthquakes, particularly the Hanshin-Awaji earthquake.

National Museum of Nuclear Science and History
601 Eubank Blvd SE, Albuquerque, NM 87123
505-245-2137
http://www.nuclearmuseum.org
This museum aims to show visitors the history of nuclear science and how it affects our lives today.

Pacific Tsunami Warning Center
91-270 Fort Weaver Rd, Ewa Beach, HI 96706-2928 USA
808-689-8207
http://www.prh.noaa.gov/ptwc
This center tracks movement of the Earth, and notifies people if a tsunami might hit from the Pacific Ocean.

Source Notes

Chapter 1. March 11, 2011

1. "Eyewitness Account of the Japanese Quake." *National Public Radio*. National Public Radio, 11 Mar. 2011. Web. 29 June 2011.

2. Ariel Zirulnick. "Japan earthquake: Eyewitness accounts capture Japan's tsunami after earthquake." *Christian Science Monitor.* The Christian Science Monitor, 11 Mar. 2011. Web. 29 June 2011.

3. "Eyewitness Accounts of Quake and Tsunami in Japan." *CTV News.* BellMedia, 11 Mar. 2011. Web. 30 June 2011.

4. Jonathan Watts. "Japan earthquake: Rescue provides rare light amid deepening darkness." *Guardian.co.uk*. Guardian News and Media Limited, 14 Mar. 2011. Web. 30 June 2011.

5. Ariel Zirulnick. "Japan earthquake: Eyewitness accounts capture Japan's tsunami after earthquake." *Christian Science Monitor.* The Christian Science Monitor, 11 Mar. 2011. Web. 29 June 2011.

6. Jonathan Watts. "Japan earthquake: Rescue provides rare light amid deepening darkness." *Guardian.co.uk*. Guardian News and Media Limited, 14 Mar. 2011. Web. 30 June 2011.

7. "Eyewitness Accounts of Quake and Tsunami in Japan." *CTV News.* BellMedia, 11 Mar. 2011. Web. 30 June 2011.

Chapter 2. A History of Disaster

1. Christine Gibson. *Smithsonian Extreme Natural Disasters*. New York: HarperCollins, 2007. Print. 201. Print.

2. Lewis H. Lapham, ed. *The End of the World*. New York: St Martin's. 1997. Print. 222. Print.

Chapter 3. After the Earth Shook

1. Kenneth Chang. "Quake Moves Japan Closer to U.S. and Alters Earth's Spin. *The New York Times.* The New York Times Company, 13 May 2011. Web. 30 June 2011.

2. "Japanese Tsunami and Earthquake." *Guardian.co.uk*. Guardian News and Media Limited, 12 Mar. 2011. Web. 30 June 2011.

3. David S. Abraham. "In Tokyo, the Search for Solid Ground." *The New York Times*. The New York Times Company, 11 Mar. 2011. Web. 30 June 2011.

4. "Japan's Survivors." *Guardian.co.uk*. Guardian News and Media Limited, 12 Mar. 2011. Web. 30 June 2011.

5. Ibid.

6. Martin Fackler. "Powerful Quake and Tsunami Devastate Northern Japan." *The New York Times.* The New York Times Company, 11 Mar. 2011. Web. 30 June 2011.

7. Ibid.

Chapter 4. Swept Out to Sea

1. "Historic Earthquakes: Sanriku Japan 1896." *USGS.* US Department of the Interior and US Geological Survey, 29 Mar. 2010. Web. 1 July 2011.

2. Todd Pitman. "American Teacher Caught in Tsunami." *Boston.com.* The New York Times Company, 16 Mar. 2011. Web. 1 July 2011.

3. Justin McCurry. "Japan tsunami survivor Hiromitsu Shinkawa found 10 miles out at sea." *Guardian.co.uk.* Guardian News and Media Limited, 13 Mar. 2011. Web. 1 July 2011.

4. David Batty. "Japan Nuclear Alert and Earthquake." *Guardian.co.uk.* Guardian News and Media Limited, 12 Mar. 2011. Web. 1 July 2011.

Chapter 5. A Nuclear Nightmare

1. Hiroko Tabuchi, et al. "Nuclear Crisis Grows for a Stricken Japan After Radiation Spews From a Reactor Fire." *The New York Times.* The New York Times Company, 15 Mar. 2011. Web. 1 July 2011.

Chapter 6. An Escalating Crisis

1. "Japan—Earthquake, Tsunami and Nuclear Crisis." *The New York Times.* The New York Times Company, 20 June 2011. Web. 1 July 2011.

2. Hiroko Tabuchi. "Japan's Nuclear Disaster Severs Town's Economic Lifeline, Setting Evacuees Adrift." *The New York Times.* The New York Times Company, 2 Apr. 2011. Web. 1 July 2011.

3. "Fukushima Accident 2011." *Word Nuclear Association.* World Nuclear Association, 30 June 2011. Web. 1 July 2011.

4. William J. Broad. "Scientists Project Path of Radiation Plume." *The New York Times.* The New York Times Company, 16 Mar. 2011. Web. 1 July 2011.

SOURCE NOTES CONTINUED

5. "About NRC." *U.S.NRC*. Nuclear Regulatory Commission, 2011. Web. 1 July 2011.

6. William J. Broad. "Scientists Project Path of Radiation Plume." *The New York Times*. The New York Times Company, 16 Mar. 2011. Web. 1 July 2011.

Chapter 7. The World Responds

1. Liz Ford and Claire Provost. "Japan Earthquake: Aid flows in from across the world." *Guardian.co.uk*. Guardian News and Media Limited, 14 Mar. 2011. Web. 1 July 2011.

2. Aimee Hurd. "Helping in Japan through One Disaster Response Worker's Eyes." *Breaking Christian News*. Breaking Christian News, 23 Mar. 2011. Web. 1 July 2011.

3. "NRC Experts Deploy To Japan As Part Of U.S. Government Response." *NRC News*. NCR, 1 Mar. 2011. Web. 1 July 2011,

4. Craig Welch. "Radiation likely from Japan found in Spokane milk." *The Seattle Times*. The Seattle Times Company, 30 Mar. 2011. Web. 1 July 2011.

5. "Bedford company to send iRobots to aid in Japan." *whdh.com*. Sunbeam Television Corp., 18 Mar. 2011. Web. 1 July 2011.

Chapter 8. Contamination

1. Hiroko Tabuchi and Ken Belson. "Contaminated Water Escaping Nuclear Plant, Japanese Regulator Warns." *The New York Times*. The New York Times Company, 28 Mar. 2011. Web. 1 July 2011.

2. CNN Wire Staff. "Japan restricts milk, vegetables produced near damaged nuclear plant." *CNN*. Cable News Network, 20 Mar. 2011. Web. 1 July 2011.

3. Simeon Bennett and Yuriy Humber. "Japan Churns Through 'Heroic' Workers Hitting Radiation Limits for Humans." *Bloomberg*. Bloomberg L.P., 18 Mar. 2011. Web. 1 July 2011.

4. "Japan—Earthquake, Tsunami and Nuclear Crisis." *The New York Times*. The New York Times Company, 20 June 2011. Web. 1 July 2011.

5. Krista Maher. "What Fukushima's Triple Meltdown Means." *Time*. Time Inc., 24 May 2011. Web. 1 July 2011.

6. "Japan—Earthquake, Tsunami and Nuclear Crisis." *The New York Times*. The New York Times Company, 20 June 2011. Web. 1 July 2011.

7. Ibid.

8. Yuri Kageyama. "Evacuees Slam Japan Nuclear Plant Operator." *Time*. Time Inc., 13 Apr. 2011. Web. 1 July 2011.

Chapter 9. Aftermath

1. "Dust Control Steps Up at Fukushima." *World Nuclear News*. n.p., Apr. 2011. Web. 1 July 2011.

2. Krista Mahr. "Fresh Concerns Emerge as Japan Unveils Timetable for Fukushima Shut Down." *Time*. Time Inc., 18 Apr. 2011. Web. 1 July 2011.

3. Jeannine Stein. "For earthquake and tsunami survivors in Japan, the psychological consequences can linger." *Los Angeles Times*. Los Angeles Times, 11 Mar. 2011. Web. 1 July 2011.

4. Ibid.

5. Damian Grammaticas. "Tsunami: Death and survival at school swimming club." *BBS News*. BCC, 15 Apr. 2011. Web. 1 July 2011.

6. Hannah Beech. "Aftermath: How Japan Will Recover from the Quake." *Time*. Time Inc., 20 Mar. 2011. Web. 1 July 2011.

INDEX

About the Author

Marcia Amidon Lusted has written more than 50 books and hundreds of magazine articles for young readers. She is also an assistant editor for Cobblestone Publishing, a writing instructor, and a musician. She lives in New Hampshire.

Photo Credits

Kyodo/AP Images, cover, 3, 6, 26, 74, 84; MPAK/Alamy, 9; The Asahi Shimbun/Getty Images, 15; Hulton Archive/Getty Images, 16, 96 (top); Red Line Editorial 20, 55; Park Ji-ho/Yonhap/AP Images, 25; Noboru Hashimoto/AFP/Getty Images, 31, 97; The Yomiuri Shimbun/AP Images, 33, 36, 65, 69, 90, 95, 98; XINHUA/Gamma-Rapho/Getty Images, 35; AP Images, 40, 46, 99 (top); Mark Baker/AP Images, 45; Gregory Bull/AP Images, 52; Itsuo Inouye/AP Images, 56, 96 (bottom); Jeff J. Daly/Alamy, 63; Koji Sasahara/AP Images, 66, 81, 83, 99 (bottom); Kyodo News/AP Images, 73